About Mastering Basic Skills—Grammar:

Welcome to Rainbow Bridge Publishing's Mastering Basic Skills—Grammar series, grade three. Mastering grammar skills builds confidence and enhances a student's entire educational experience. This workbook is designed to help students understand and master sentence construction and fundamental grammatical principles. It both reinforces classroom skills and gets students well on their way to reading and writing independently and competently, and it is ideal for use during or after school.

By making a connection between their previous language experience and the ideas in the text, students realize they have already learned a number of key grammar concepts. Based on NCTE (National Council of Teachers of English) standards and core curriculum, this workbook helps students understand basic sentence patterns, beginning with subject and predicate. They build on this foundation by completing exercises and games that teach parts of speech, verb tense and number, agreement, sentence types and punctuation. By continually relating workbook concepts to their existing knowledge, students learn to recognize correct grammar and construct their own sentences.

This workbook holds the students' interest with a mix of humor, imagination and instruction. The diverse assignments teach proper use of adjectives and adverbs while also giving students something fun to think about—from kangaroos to Clara Barton. As students complete the workbook, they will be well prepared to master additional language skills related to word choice, meaning, intent and audience.

Nothing is more basic to a solid education than reading and writing. This workbook helps students enhance both skills, strengthening students' confidence, helping them enjoy language and ultimately encouraging them to read and write on their own.

Rainbow Bridge Publishing
www.summerbridgeactivities.com
www.rbpbooks.com

Table of Contents

Mr. Fredrickson's Spaceship

Name _____ Date _____

◇Start Here!

Read each sentence. Circle the subject or subjects of each sentence.

The <u>subject</u> is the part of the sentence that names the person, place, or thing the sentence is about. A sentence can have one subject or more than one.

Example: Mr. Fredrickson and the principal marched into the room.

---

1 Mr. Fredrickson is our very tall teacher.

2 He reads us books about the solar system.

3 Mercury and Venus are close to the sun.

4 We saw a video about the moon.

5 Astronauts went to the moon in 1969.

6 Mr. Fredrickson decided to build a spaceship right in our school.

7 The spaceship has windows and seats like a real spaceship.

8 Julie and Jake Smith were chosen as the first student astronauts.

9 The principal gave them radios to use.

10 Another student gave them instructions over the radio.

11 They ate lunch right in the spaceship.

12 At the end of the day, Julie and Jake's parents came to see.

13 Mrs. Smith said over the radio, "Please return to Earth."

Gee whiz, Mr. Fredrickson, you're really tall!

Matt's Turn to Be an Astronaut

Name _____ Date _____

◇ Start Here!

Read each sentence. Circle the predicate.

The <u>predicate</u> tells what happens in the sentence.

Example: Mr. Fredrickson and the principal (marched into the room.)

1 Mr. Fredrickson chose two new students as astronauts.

2 Matt and Jeff said good-bye to the class.

3 They took their books, their notebooks, and their lunches.

4 The principal gave them the radios to use.

5 They went into the spaceship.

6 Another student told them to prepare for blastoff.

7 They buckled their seat belts.

8 The principal counted, "Ten, nine, eight, seven, six, five, four, three, two, one."

9 The other students shouted, "Blast off!"

10 Over the radio, Mr. Fredrickson said, "Come in, astronauts."

11 Jeff answered over the radio.

12 Mr. Fredrickson asked how far away the sun was from the earth.

13 Matt answered, "Ninety-three million miles."

Name _____ Date _____

◇ Start Here!

Study this map. Then write five statements about it. Remember to start with a capital letter and end with a period.

A <u>statement</u> is a sentence that tells something. It starts with a capital letter and ends with a period.

Example: New York is close to the Atlantic Ocean.

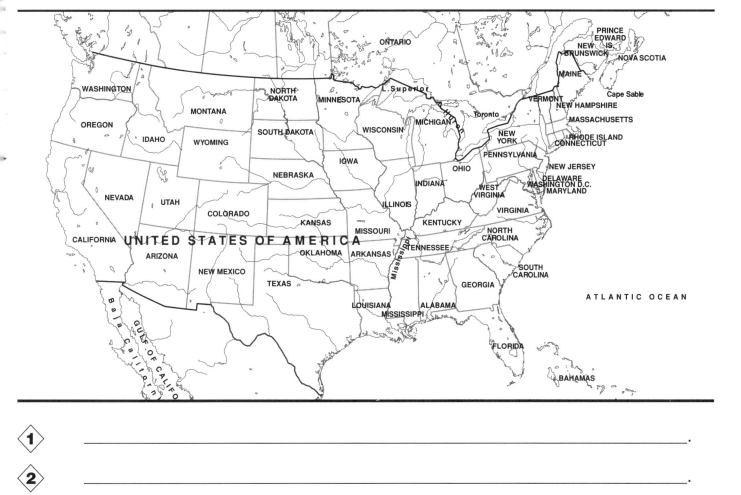

1. _____.

2. _____.

3. _____.

4. _____.

5. _____.

 Denise's Great Idea: Draw a star on the map to show where you live.

The Third President of the United States

Name _____ Date _____

◇ **Start Here!**

After each group of words, write "complete" if the sentence is complete. If the sentence is not complete, add words to make it a complete sentence.

A sentence has a subject, a predicate, and a complete idea. The subject tells who or what the sentence is about. The predicate includes the verb and words that help make the verb complete.

Examples: <u>Mr. Fredrickson store.</u>
This sentence has a subject but not a predicate or complete idea.
<u>Mr. Fredrickson went to the store.</u>
This sentence has a subject (Mr. Fredrickson), a predicate (went to the store) and a complete idea.

1 Thomas Jefferson lived in Virginia.

_____

2 Had a home called Monticello.

_____

3 He loved to do science experiments right in his home.

_____

4 He collected many books for his library.

_____

5 Books about history.

_____

6 Thomas Jefferson books about geometry.

_____

Name _____ Date _____

◇ Start Here!

Study these drawings of coins. Then write five questions. Remember to start with a capital letter and end with a question mark.

A <u>question</u> is a sentence that asks something. It starts with a capital letter and ends with a question mark.

Example: How many quarters are there?

① _____

② _____

③ _____

④ _____

⑤ _____

 Denise's Great Idea: What could you buy with this much money?

Name _____ Date _____

Use the phrases in the box to make up funny exclamations. Remember to end with an exclamation point.

A sentence that shows excitement or strong feeling is an <u>exclamation</u>. It starts with a capital letter and ends with an exclamation point.

Example: Hurry up! The movie is starting!

behind you	in your hair	on your arm
eating your lunch	on the teacher	in your backpack

1 Look out! There's a spider _____

2 Watch out! There's a monster _____

3 Wow! I see an elephant _____

4 I don't believe it! the President is _____

5 Oh, no! I see a space alien _____

6 Look at that! Your friend is _____

This exercise is so exciting!!

Name _____   Date _____

◇ Start Here!

Write three commands your teacher might give you.

A sentence that tells someone to do something is a <u>command</u>. It begins with a capital letter and ends with a period.

Example: Take out the garbage.

___

1 _____

2 _____

3 _____

Write three polite commands you might use while eating dinner with your family.

1 _____

2 _____

3 _____

Name _____ Date _____

◇ Start Here!

Read each sentence and write whether it is a statement, question, exclamation or command. Then add a period, question mark or exclamation mark.

Example: Do you like your lunch? _____**question**_____

1 Matt's dog followed him to school _____

2 Oh no, the dog is chasing the principal _____

3 What is that dog doing here _____

4 Please take your dog home _____

Using phrases in the box, write your own statement, question, exclamation and command.

a one-eyed, purple people eater	potatoes and gravy
a substitute teacher	snow on the sidewalk

1 _____

2 _____

3 _____

4 _____

Name _____ Date _____

◇ **Start Here!**

In this sea of words, circle the nouns.

A <u>noun</u> is a word that names a person, place or thing.

run   balloon

hat   book

cookie

pretty

blue

school   cat

answer   river   park   powerful

growl   blanket   build   is   fiddle

guitar   faint   about

beach   airport   announce   shark

happy   eyebrow   next   insect

Name _____ Date _____

◇ Start Here!

Circle the proper nouns in these sentences and underline the common nouns.

A <u>common</u> <u>noun</u> names an ordinary person, place or thing. A <u>proper</u> <u>noun</u> begins with a capital letter and names a particular person, place, or thing.

---

1 (Galileo) was a famous <u>astronomer</u> who lived about four hundred <u>years</u> ago.

2 Galileo was born in Italy in a town called Pisa.

3 When he was a boy, Galileo loved to do math problems.

4 As a young man, Galileo studied to become a doctor.

5 But Galileo loved to see the stars at night and our galaxy, the Milky Way.

6 Galileo built a telescope so he could watch the moon and stars.

7 The planet Jupiter is the largest planet in our solar system.

8 Galileo discovered four moons revolving around Jupiter.

9 Venus is the closest planet to Earth.

10 Galileo also made important discoveries about Venus.

11 Galileo died near the city of Florence in 1642.

 Denise's Great idea: Can you name another famous scientist?

Name That Plural

Name _____ Date _____

◇ Start Here!

Make these nouns plural by following the directions below.

A <u>singular</u> <u>noun</u> names one thing. A <u>plural</u> <u>noun</u> names more than one. To make the plural of most nouns, add <u>s</u>. For nouns that end in <u>s</u>, <u>sh</u>, <u>ch</u>, or <u>x</u>, make the plural by adding <u>es</u>. For nouns that end with a consonant and <u>y</u>, make the plural by changing the <u>y</u> to <u>i</u> and adding <u>es</u>.

Examples:
boy	boys
church	churches
story	stories

1 zebra _____ 2 princess _____

3 horse _____ 4 mushroom _____

5 watch _____ 6 shovel _____

7 ax _____ 8 tuba _____

9 mammal _____ 10 peach _____

11 giraffe _____ 12 hotel _____

13 dolphin _____ 14 sandwich _____

15 wish _____ 16 carrot _____

16 alligator _____ 17 candy _____

17 bandage _____ 18 arrow _____

Hilarious Animals

Name _____ Date _____

◇Start Here!

Make the plural by choosing a word from the box.

To form the plurals of some nouns, you use the same word as the singular or a new word.

Example: child   children
               deer   deer

---

geese	mice	elk	oxen
fish	wolves	sheep	buffalo

1. The (goose) _____ ate ice cream.

2. The (wolf) _____ read a book.

3. The (buffalo) _____ had a tea party.

4. The (mouse) _____ played a video game.

5. The (sheep) _____ went to a movie.

6. The (elk) _____ went to the barber shop.

7. The (ox) _____ played on the swings.

8. The (fish) _____ played hopscotch.

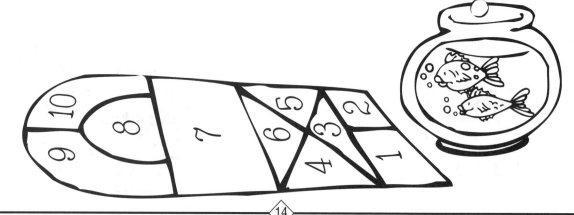

Name _____ Date _____

◇Start Here!

Circle the plural nouns in these sentences. Draw a line under the proper nouns.

1. Australia is famous for kangaroos, furry animals that hop on their hind legs.

2. Kangaroos also live in New Guinea.

3. Kangaroos like to eat grass and leaves.

4. Matt's family and several other people flew to New Zealand.

5. Next they went to Australia, the only country that is also a continent.

6. Matt and the other children were excited to see kangaroos.

7. Kangaroos have heads like deer but legs likes rabbits.

8. On the way to the Simpson Desert, Matt saw a large group of red kangaroos called a mob.

9. Near the Murray River, some of the kangaroos hopped six feet high.

10. The babies peeked out from their mothers' pouches.

11. At the city of Sydney, Matt and his parents bought a special book about kangaroos.

Name _____ Date _____

◇ Start Here!

Think about what happens at recess. Then write as many verbs as you can to describe recess.

A <u>verb</u> is a word that shows action.

Examples: run   shout

_____   _____

_____   _____

_____   _____

_____   _____

_____   _____

_____   _____

_____   _____

_____   _____

That's pretty sneaky, getting us to do grammar during recess!

Name _____   Date _____

◇ **Start Here!**

Write the correct verb in the blank by choosing a word from the box.

Some verbs don't show action. Instead, they tell about something. They are called <u>state</u>-<u>of</u>-<u>being</u> or <u>to</u> <u>be</u> verbs.

Example: My cat <u>is</u> funny.

is	am	are	was	were

1. A banyan tree _____ a very interesting plant.

2. One banyan tree _____ like a small forest because it has many trunks.

3. I learned about them when I _____ little.

4. Now that I _____ older, I want to see a banyan tree.

5. Then my dad surprised me when he said we _____ going to India.

6. Many relatives _____ at the airport when we left.

7. India _____ a country that has more people than any country except China.

8. Much of India _____ a huge peninsula.

9. There _____ many banyan trees in India.

10. My mother _____ happy when Dad and I came home.

11. I _____ very glad we got to see the great banyan in Calcutta.

I Would Live in a Tree House

Name _____   Date _____

◇ **Start Here!**

Complete the sentences below by choosing helping verbs from the box.

Some action verbs need help from another verb to be complete. These are called <u>helping</u> <u>verbs</u>.

Example: He <u>is</u> <u>running</u> hard.

am	have	can	do	would
does	was	are	is	might

1 Human beings _____ built houses for thousands of years.

2 Long ago, dried mud _____ used to construct Indian houses.

3 Strange looking houseboats _____ found in Hong Kong.

4 Today, a typical house _____ made of wood or brick.

5 Eskimos _____ shape houses out of ice.

6 Many people _____ live in apartment buildings.

7 My friend _____ not want to live in a log cabin.

8 I _____ hoping to build my own house someday.

9 I _____ build it by the ocean.

10 I _____ draw a picture of it after school.

 Denise's Great Idea: If you could build your own house, what kind would you build?

Name _____ Date _____

◇ Start Here!

Create past-tense verbs for the sentences by following the example below.

Present-tense verbs tell about something that is happening now. Past-tense verbs tell about something that has already happened. To make most verbs past tense, just add ed. For a verb that ends in e, drop the final e and add ed. For verbs that end in a consonant followed by y, change the y to i and add ed.

Examples: walk   walk + ed   = walked
            skate   skate-e + ed   = skated
            copy   copy-y + i + ed   = copied

 1 Last year we (study) _____ about fire.

 2 We (learn) _____ that fire requires three things: fuel, heat and oxygen.

 3 Long ago, people (discover) _____ they could keep warm with fire.

 4 They also (cook) _____ food with fire.

 5 They searched for wood and (carry) _____ it back to their homes.

 6 In our class, we (regulate) _____ a fire by controlling fuel and oxygen.

 7 A man named John Walker (invent) _____ the first match in 1827.

8 He (mix) _____ several chemicals to create the match.

We cook over a fire when we go camping!

Name _____ Date _____

◇Start Here!

Choose words from the box to complete this story.

Some past-tense verbs do not end with <u>ed</u>. These are called <u>irregular</u> <u>verbs</u>.

did	wrote	thought	was	told
heard	gave	began	gave	took

Clara Barton (is) _____ a famous nurse. During the Civil War, she (hear) _____ that wounded soldiers needed help. She (do) _____ many good things for them. She (write) _____ letters for them and (give) _____ them medicine. She (take) _____ blankets to them.

After the war, she (think) _____ it would be good to help more people. She (tell) _____ others about her ideas. In 1881, she (begin) _____ the American Red Cross. The Red Cross (give) _____ help to hungry, sick and injured individuals. Today, the Red Cross helps people after fires, earthquakes and other disasters.

Clara Barton was a hero!

Name _____ Date _____

◇ Start Here!

Choose the correct verb.

Present-tense action verbs that tell about one person, place, animal or thing have <u>s</u> or <u>es</u> added to the end. Present-tense action verbs that tell about more than one thing stay the same.

Example: Mr. Fredrickson teach + es = <u>teaches</u> us about skeletons.
                   The students <u>read</u> their books.

1. Mr. Fredrickson (bring, brings) a plastic skeleton to class.

2. We (call, calls) him Mr. Bones.

3. Mr. Bones (hang, hangs) in the corner of the classroom.

4. When the students arrive, they all (say, says),
"Good morning, Mr. Bones."

5. Many bones (link, links) together to form a skeleton.

6. Blood vessels (take, takes) blood to the bones.

7. A hinge joint, like an elbow, (move, moves) in one
direction.

8. A ball-and-socket joint (allow, allows) the hip to swing
in both directions.

9. As a baby (grow, grows), cartilage slowly changes
to bone.

10. Living bones (bend, bends) slightly.

11. The principal says, "Hello, Mr. Bones" and
(shake, shakes) the skeleton's hand.

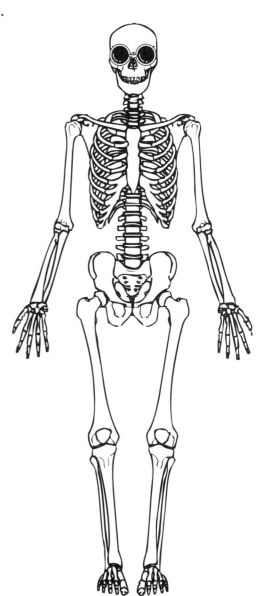

Wonderful Wheels

Name _____ Date _____

◇ Start Here!

Write the correct form of the verb in the blank.

1. Before the wheel was invented, people (drag, dragged) _____ heavy loads over the ground.

2. We are not sure who (invents, invented) _____ the first wheel.

3. Wooden wheels for carts first (appear, appeared) _____ about five thousand years ago.

4. A few hundred years later, people (begin, began) _____ to use wheels with spokes.

5. Today, the gyroscope (is, was) _____ a special wheel used in airplanes and ships.

6. Gyroscopes (help, helped) _____ vehicles move in the right direction.

7. Bicycle tires are comfortable wheels because they (are, were) _____ filled with air.

8. The bar that holds your bicycle tire in place (is, was) _____ called the axle.

Name _____   Date _____

Write the possessive forms of the nouns below. Then create your own story by choosing which phrase you would like to add to the sentences.

A <u>possessive</u> <u>noun</u> shows that someone or something owns or has something. You make a noun possessive by adding <u>'s</u>.

Example: The <u>student's</u> pencil was orange with blue stripes.

My friend ___ name is Andrea. Her yard is next to an old house. She says the house is haunted. The house ___ grass is tall and full of weeds. When it was dark, we borrowed her dad ___ flashlight. We walked through the tall grass to the house. We went inside. All of a sudden, we heard _____.

a loud scream   someone coming toward us   a voice call our names

Andrea ___ hand began to shake. She dropped the flashlight. The flashlight ___ batteries fell out. We stumbled in the darkness. We felt for the door. Finally we found the door ___ handle. We ran out _____.

and never went back   and returned the next night   and told our parents

www.rbpbooks.com   reproducible   **MBS—Grammar Grade 3**

Name _____ Date _____

◇**Start Here!**

See if you can find all the pronouns in this story. Write them at the bottom.

A <u>pronoun</u> takes the place of a noun.

Examples: Mr. Fredrickson is a good teacher.   <u>He</u> is a good teacher.
That ball field is big.   <u>It</u> is big.

Veterinarians receive a special education to become animal doctors. They take care of all kinds of animals, including horses, dogs, cats, and chickens. Aunt Ruby is a veterinarian. She has an office nearby. When our dog Rusty got sick, Dad was worried. He said we should take Rusty to Aunt Ruby. She gave Rusty some medicine. It worked.

We saw several people at the office. They all had pets. We saw two dogs, one cat, and one parrot. Aunt Ruby is a good vet. She is very kind to the animals. Dad is glad Rusty is better. Now when he throws the ball, Rusty brings the ball back.

1. _____   2. _____   3. _____

4. _____   5. _____   6. _____

7. _____   8. _____   9. _____

10. _____   11. _____   12. _____

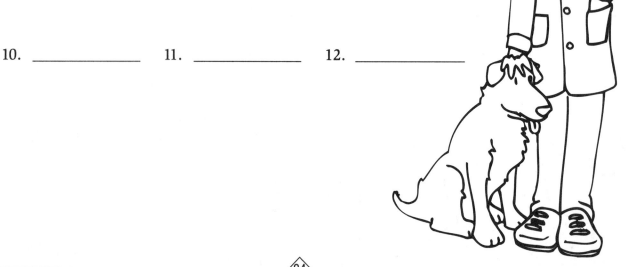

Name _____ Date _____

◇ Start Here!

Write in the object pronouns in this story.

Some pronouns that take the place of nouns are used with words like <u>of</u>, <u>to</u>, <u>over</u>, <u>with</u>, and <u>about</u>. These are called <u>object</u> <u>pronouns</u>.

Example: I went with Mr. Fredrickson.   I went with <u>him</u>.

| him | her | them | it | you | me | us |

My grandparents lived during the Great Depression. It was a very difficult time for

_____. My grandpa had a farm in Oklahoma. His father gave it to _____. My grandma

moved to Oklahoma when she was twenty years old. Two years later, my grandpa married

_____. They worked hard in the field, but strong winds blew huge clouds of dust over

_____. The crops died, and the region became known as the Dust Bowl.

They had to move to California. They worked hard picking fruit. Saving money was hard

for _____. But after my dad was born, they saved money for _____. He was able to

attend college.

My family visits my grandparents every Christmas. They tell _____what life was like in

Oklahoma. I would like to see the area that was called the Dust Bowl. That would be interesting to

_____. Have your grandparents ever told _____ about the Great Depression?

www.rbpbooks.com   reproducible   **MBS—Grammar Grade 3**

Name _____ Date _____

◇**Start Here!**

In these sentences, choose the right possessive pronoun.

Possessive pronouns take the place of possessive nouns. They show that someone or something owns or has something.

Example: Mr. Fredrickson's spaceship is a lot of fun.   His spaceship is a lot of fun.

---

1 Today I went to (my, me) _____ dentist.

2 (She, Her) _____ office has an aquarium.

3 One fish stayed inside a castle. That fish liked (its, their) _____ castle.

4 (I, My) _____ tooth was bothering me. The dentist took an X-ray.

5 She said (my, our) _____ X-ray showed a cavity.

6 Kyle, (her, she) assistant, gave me a shot. It didn't hurt.

7 Then Kyle sat down in (him, his) _____ chair.

8 He helped the dentist while she filled (my, me) tooth.

9 I could feel (their, they) _____ rubber gloves inside my mouth.

10 "All done," said the dentist. (Me, My) _____ mouth felt good.

11 My brothers and I all like (our, us) _____ dentist.

12 You can take care of (their, your) teeth by brushing regularly.

Brush your teeth every day, and you'll prevent tooth decay!

Two Sentences Magically Become One ☆

Name _____ Date _____

⬦ **Start Here!**

Combine sentences by choosing the right pronoun.

1 Astronauts went to the moon in 1969. Astronauts walked on the moon's surface.

Astronauts went to the moon in 1969, and (them, they) _____ walked on

(its, their) _____ surface.

2 Mr. Fredrickson built a spaceship right in our school. Mr. Fredrickson got radios for the students to use.

Mr. Fredrickson built a spaceship right in our school, and (he, him) _____ got radios

for (we, us) _____ to use.

3 My mom and I went to the movie *Tarzan*. My mom and I ate hot buttered popcorn while we watched *Tarzan*.

My mom and I went to the movie *Tarzan*, and (they, we) _____ ate hot buttered pop-

corn while we watched (it, them) _____ .

Use pronouns to combine these two sentences.

Julie and Jake were the first student astronauts. Julie and Jake went into the spaceship.

_____

_____

Name _____ Date _____

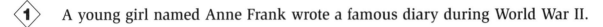

◇**Start Here!**

Circle the adjectives in these sentences.

An <u>adjective</u> describes a noun.

Examples: (famous) authors   (blue) sky   (fun) game   (hard) test

1 A young girl named Anne Frank wrote a famous diary during World War II.

2 E. B. White wrote a wonderful book called *Charlotte's Web*.

3 Many people consider Shakespeare the perfect writer.

4 Mary Wollstonecraft Shelley was a brilliant writer who wrote a scary story called *Frankenstein*.

5 Robert Louis Stevenson is the author of an exciting story called *Treasure Island*.

6 Dr. Seuss wrote funny stories and imaginative poems.

7 My favorite book by Beverly Cleary is *Ramona Quimby: Age 8*.

8 Laura Ingalls Wilder wrote important books about a little house on a pleasant prairie.

9 Mark Twain was a humorous author and a serious author. He wrote a memorable book called *Huckleberry Finn*.

Can you guess my favorite book?

Name _____ Date _____

◇ Start Here!

Circle the correct adjective in these sentences.

Adjectives that compare two things usually end in <u>er</u>. Adjectives that compare more than two things usually end in <u>est</u>.

Examples: My bike is <u>faster</u> than your bike.

            This painting is the <u>prettiest</u> one in the museum.

1   My clay monster is the (ugly, uglier, ugliest) in the whole class.

2   At recess, Denise kicked the ball (high, higher, highest) into the air.

3   Mr. Fredrickson, our funny teacher, kicked it (high, higher, highest) than Denise.

4   Mrs. Clark, our stern principal, kicked it (high, higher, highest).

5   Her high-heel shoe went flying (farther, farthest) than the ball.

6   About a hundred kids went running after her shoe. Tommy ran the (fast, faster, fastest). We call him Tommy the Terrible.

7   Tommy the Terrible dove for the shoe in a pool of mud. He got (dirty, dirtier, dirtiest) than his friend.

8   Then he brought back the shoe. Everyone laughed. Mrs. Clark laughed the (hard, harder, hardest).

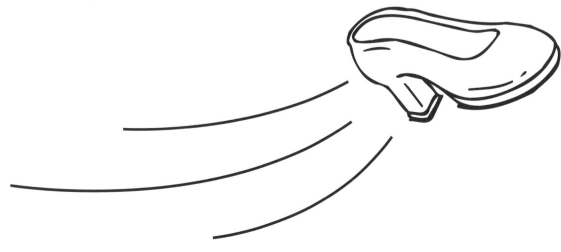

Name _____   Date _____

◇ Start Here!

Choose an adverb from the box and write it in the blank.

<u>Adverbs</u> describe verbs. They often end in <u>ly</u>.

Example: It was raining <u>lightly</u>.

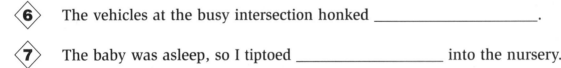

heavily	wildly	loudly	brightly
quietly	quickly	carefully	timidly

1 I looked at the glorious Milky Way. The stars were shining _____.

2 When the vicious dog barked, my cat jumped _____ into the tree.

3 Mr. Fredrickson, our intelligent instructor, spoke _____ into the intercom.

4 He said that it had snowed _____ that day.

5 When he said there would be no school tomorrow, the students cheered _____.

6 The vehicles at the busy intersection honked _____.

7 The baby was asleep, so I tiptoed _____ into the nursery.

8 I _____ put the bandage on my cut finger.

My Dinosaur Buddies

Name _____ Date _____

◇ Start Here!

Circle the correct word in these sentences.

Do you know the difference between <u>good</u> and <u>well</u>? <u>Good</u> is an adjective that describes nouns. <u>Well</u> is an adverb that describes verbs.

Examples: My pet tyrannosaurus rex is a good dinosaur. (<u>Good</u> describes the dinosaur.)

He did well in the pet show. (<u>Well</u> tells how the pet did.)

1. My dinosaur's name is Mr. Rex. He has (good, well) teeth.

2. I tell Mr. Rex to chew his food (good, well).

3. Mr. Rex is 70 million years old. That's a (good, well) age.

4. Mr. Rex has a (good, well) friend named Dr. Diplodocus.

5. Dr. Diplodocus has a long tail and does not run too (good, well).

6. He searches for (good, well) leaves to eat.

7. I can ride pretty (good, well) on my protoceratops.

8. Her name is Profound Progenitor. I think it's a (good, well) name.

9. Yesterday we all had a (good, well) party.

Name _____ Date _____

Circle the correct word in these sentences.

Use <u>a</u> with words that start with consonant sounds. Use <u>an</u> with words that start with vowel sounds.

Examples: I ate <u>an</u> apple.   I rode <u>a</u> bike.

---

1. New Zealand has been (a, an) independent country since 1907.

2. The capital city of Wellington is (a, an) busy port.

3. The kiwi is (a, an) interesting looking bird that cannot fly.

4. Some workers in New Zealand can shear (a, an) sheep in less than a minute.

5. The Maori people have (a, an) fascinating tradition of greeting each other by rubbing noses.

6. New Zealand has (a, an) active volcano called Ruapehu.

7. South Island has (a, an) group of beautiful mountains called the Southern Alps.

8. North Island has (a, an) larger population than South Island.

The kiwi doesn't look like any other bird I've ever seen!

Name _____ Date _____

◇ Start Here!

Choose the correct word in these sentences.

Do not follow a <u>negative</u> (such as <u>not</u>) with a second negative. Use the word <u>no</u> to describe a noun. Use the word <u>none</u> by itself.

Examples: I don't have no toys. (Incorrect—this is a double negative.)

I don't have any toys. (Correct)

I have none.

1. I peeked in the cookie jar. We didn't have (no, any) cookies.

2. I glanced in the fridge. We had (no, none) milk.

3. I checked the cupboard for bread. We had (no, none).

4. I looked in the drawer but did not find (none, any) soup.

5. I peered in the pantry but saw (no, none) food.

6. I stared at the shelf, but there wasn't (nothing, anything) there.

7. "I'm hungry," I said, but (none, no one) heard me. Then I remembered the freezer.

8. There were (no, none) cookies inside, but there was a lot of ice cream.

9. I ate some delicious banana nut ice cream but didn't use (no, a) bowl.

10. Then I didn't want (any, no) dinner.

 Denise's Great Idea: What is your favorite flavor of ice cream?

Name _____ Date _____

◇ Start Here!

Match the words in the box to the synonym below.

A <u>synonym</u> is a word with a similar meaning to another word.

Example: I <u>walked</u> to school. I <u>strolled</u> to school.

---

yell	small	flame	inexpensive	complain
chide	assist	glimmer	name	big

shout   _____

gripe   _____

large   _____

fire   _____

cheap   _____

little   _____

scold   _____

help   _____

title   _____

glisten   _____

Name _____ Date _____

◇ **Start Here!**

To change the meaning of this story, cross out the old word and replace it with an antonym from the box. Change other words, such as <u>a</u> or <u>an</u> if you need to.

An <u>antonym</u> is a word that is opposite in meaning to another word.

Example: It is <u>hot</u> outside.   It is <u>cold</u> outside.

loved	smiled	boy	friend	do
good	quiet	kind	young	Yes
brave	stay	excellent	always	

Deep in the woods there lived a mean _____ witch. She hated _____ everyone.

One fine day she was walking through her noisy _____ forest when she spied an old

_____ man _____. She asked, "What are you doing in my forest?"

"I heard you needed an enemy _____," he answered.

"No _____, I don't _____," she said.

He was scared _____ and wanted to run away _____.

The witch cast an evil _____ spell. She told him he would always have terrible

_____ luck.

The witch frowned _____. "I hope you never _____ come back," she said.

Name _____ Date _____

◇ Start Here!

For each sentence, circle the correct homophone.

A <u>homophone</u> is a word that is pronounced like another word but spelled differently.

Example: I have <u>two</u> birds.   I gave a cracker <u>to</u> my bird.

1⟩   The entire third grade went (to, too) the store.

2⟩   They walked every single (step, steppe) of the (weigh, way).

3⟩   They walked past the state (capital, capitol) building.

4⟩   The (principal, principle) bought them triple-decker ice cream cones.

5⟩   (Their, They're) ice cream cones began to melt in the hot (son, sun).

6⟩   Luckily, the good ice cream witch of the north happened to be (there, their).

7⟩   She (blue, blew) cold wind that froze the ice cream.

8⟩   "(Your, You're) a wonderful witch," said the third graders.

9⟩   "I love ice cream," she said. "(It's, Its) the most wonderful food in the world."

Name _____ Date _____

◇Start Here!

Find the <u>incomplete</u> <u>sentences</u> in this story. Circle them in red crayon.

Davy Crockett in Tennessee in 1786. A song about him said he killed a bear when he was only three. He loved to fish and hunt and spend time in the woods. He ran away from home when he was thirteen and did not come back for two years. Parents very glad.

Davy was a famous frontiersman. People used to say he could "run faster, jump higher, squat lower, dive deeper, and stay under longer than any man in the whole country." Elected to Congress. Davy had an interesting motto. "Be always sure you're right," he said, "then go ahead."

When he was almost fifty years old. Davy rode his horse all the way to Texas. Met two other famous men, Jim Bowie and William Travis. Jim had invented a famous hunting knife called the Bowie knife. William had been a school teacher in Alabama. They joined 186 other men who wanted freedom from Mexico.

Davy, Jim, William, and the others fought against 4,000 Mexican soldiers at a place called the Alamo. The battle thirteen days. Davy and the others all died, but they became heroes. "Remember the Alamo" became a famous saying. The Texans gained their independence from Mexico.

Name _____ Date _____

◇ Start Here!

Write in the correct noun.

1 (Kite, Kites) _____ are the oldest flying machines.

2 People in (China, china) _____ learned how to fly silk (kite, kites) _____ more than 3,000 years ago.

3 One general frightened enemy (soldier, soldiers, Soldiers) _____ by flying scary kites.

4 A tight line or string allows a (kite, kites) _____ to fly.

5 (Children, Child) _____ in (Europe, europe) _____ have flown kites for more than 1,000 years.

6 The flat (kite, kites) _____ is shaped like a diamond.

7 Box kites have (frame, frames) _____ that help them fly.

8 Delta kites are shaped like (triangle, triangles) _____ and fly well in light winds.

9 An inventor from (England, england) _____ named George Cayley invented a kite large enough to carry a (people, person) _____.

Let's go fly a kite!

Name _____ Date _____

◇Start Here!

In this group of nouns, circle the ones that should be capitalized.

george	jessica	school	water
book	eagle	girl	zeus
asia	house	mount fuji	washing machine
national flag	eskimo	desert	white house
james cook	writer	castle	secret agent
virginia		mountview elementary school	

For each of these singular nouns, write the plural next to it.

woman _____

fox _____

pencil _____

catch _____

deer _____

wolf _____

shelf _____

glass _____

vase _____

Name _____ Date _____

◇Start Here!

Circle the correct verb.

1   People all over the world (like, likes) to play games.

2   My dad (enjoys, enjoyed) playing hide-and-seek when he was little.

3   Board games (was, were) invented 4,000 years ago.

4   The board originally (represents, represented) a battle site.

5   Checkers and chess (is, are) examples of board games.

6   In chess, each player (try, tries) to capture the other player's king.

7   At schools, children sometimes (gather, gathers) to play jump rope.

8   (Run, Running) is an important part of the game of tag.

9   A person playing hopscotch needs to (balance, balanced) on one foot.

10   Computer games allow you to (compete, competes) against the computer or against another player.

11   When I play my brother, he (operated, operates) the joystick very quickly.

12   I played chess against the computer, and I (win, won).

Name _____ Date _____

◇ **Start Here!**

Choose nouns and verbs. When necessary, make sure that singular nouns have singular verbs and that plural nouns have plural verbs. Add <u>a</u> or <u>an</u> if needed. Also add capital letters if needed.

---

1 "I love the solar system," (say, says) _____ our tall, tall teacher, Mr. Fredrickson.

2 (astronomer, astronomers) _____ (believe, believes) _____ that Saturn has more than twenty moons.

3 Can you (name, names) _____ a planet other than Earth that (has, have) _____ polar ice caps?

4 The answer is Mars. People used to think there (were, was) _____ canals on Mars.

5 (planet, planets) _____ (is, are) _____ spherical (object, objects) _____ that (revolve, revolves) _____ around a sun.

6 Do you know which planet (is, are) _____ the smallest?

7 The answer is Pluto. It is also the outermost planet. However, every 248 years Pluto (move, moves) _____ within Neptune's orbit.

Name _____ Date _____

◇ Start Here!

Rewrite these sentences and use pronouns in place of nouns. If possible, combine sentences.

1 Americans like hamburgers. Americans consume 15 million hamburgers every day.

_____.

2 Some people in New Zealand loved cookies. Those people made the world's biggest cookie.

_____.

3 The cookie was big enough to cover two tennis courts.

_____.

4 George Crum was an American Indian. George invented potato chips.

_____.

5 In Japan, people eat raw fish. People love raw fish.

_____.

6 Pizza is my sister's favorite. My sister even eats pizza for breakfast.

_____.

Name _____ Date _____

◇Start Here!

Circle the correct adjective or adverb.

1. Japan is (small, smaller, smallest) than the United States.

2. Japan has four main islands. The (large, larger, largest) is Honshu.

3. Japanese people travel by train (more, most) than people in other countries.

4. Tokyo is a (dense, densely) populated city of 18 million.

5. My mother speaks Japanese quite (good, well).

6. Japanese is one of the (hard, harder, hardest) languages to learn.

7. Japanese children (happy, happily) wear uniforms to school.

8. If you go to a Japanese temple, please speak (quiet, quietly).

9. Mount Fuji is a (pretty, prettily) mountain in Japan.

10. To make paper figures called origami, you need to (careful, carefully) fold the paper.

11. Many Japanese children are (good, well) baseball players.

12. The (fast, faster, fastest) train in Japan is called the bullet train.

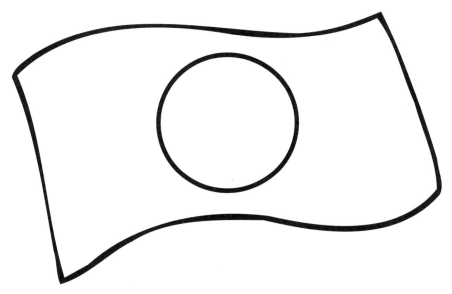

Wanted: Authors

Name _____ Date _____

◇ Start Here!

Write your own story. Use as many of these words or phrases as you need. Be sure to include at least one statement, one question, one exclamation and one command.

horse	flying	wizard	wicked witch
enchanted forest	ran like the wind		the middle of the trees
magic stone	beneath the lake	lovely	jagged
shouted	sword of steel	beautiful fairy	dashed to pieces

_____

_____

_____

_____

_____

_____

_____

_____

_____

_____

I need a big pencil for all my big ideas!

Name _____ Date _____

Combine words and phrases to make a funny story about Mr. Fredrickson. Circle the subject and verb of each sentence.

One fine day, Mr. Fredrickson came to class _____.

riding a pony   wearing a clown suit   eating a giant sucker

We were all surprised when he announced _____.

there was something scary outside   there was something funny outside

When we looked outside, we saw _____.

hungry space aliens   our principal on the slide   fifteen large giraffes

"Oh, no!" cried Mr. Fredrickson. "_____."

The Martians are coming   The principal is having too much fun

The giraffes want to have a race

We all ran outside and _____.

met the aliens   played with the principal   rode the giraffes

"Wow!" we said. "We sure are glad _____

_____."

(Make this one up yourself.)

Answer Pages

Page 3
1. Mr. Fredrickson
2. He
3. Mercury, Venus
4. We
5. Astronauts
6. Mr. Fredrickson
7. The spaceship
8. Julie, Jake Smith
9. The principal
10. Another student
11. They
12. Julie and Jake's parents
13. Mrs. Smith

Page 4
1. chose two new students as astronauts
2. said good-bye to the class
3. took their books, their notebooks, and their lunches
4. gave them the radios to use
5. went into the spaceship
6. told them to prepare for blastoff
7. buckled their seat belts
8. counted, "Ten, nine, eight, seven, six, five, four, three, two, one."
9. shouted, "Blast off!"
10. said, "Come in, astronauts."
11. answered over the radio
12. asked how far away the sun was from the earth
13. answered, "Ninety-three million miles."

Page 5
Answers will vary.

Page 6
(Answers may vary—but should be complete sentences.)
1. Complete
2. He had a home called Monticello.
3. Complete
4. Complete
5. He read books about history.
6. Thomas Jefferson read books about geography.

Page 7
Answers will vary.

Page 8
Answers will vary.

Page 9
Answers will vary.

Page 10
1. Matt's dog followed him to school.   Statement
2. Oh no, the dog is chasing the principal!   Exclamation
3. What is that dog doing here?   Question
4. Please take your dog home.   Command
1–4 Answers will vary.

Page 11

balloon	hat
book	cookie
school	cat
answer	river
park	growl
blanket	fiddle
guitar	beach
airport	shark
eyebrow	insect

Page 12
1. (Galileo) astronomer, years
2. (Galileo) (Italy) town, (Pisa)
3. boy, (Galileo) problems
4. man, (Galileo) doctor
5. (Galileo) stars, night, galaxy, (Milky Way)
6. (Galileo) telescope, moon, stars
7. planet, (Jupiter) planet, solar system
8. (Galileo) moons, (Jupiter)
9. (Venus) planet, (Earth)
10. (Galileo) discoveries, (Venus)
11. (Galileo) city, (Florence)

Page 13
1. zebras
2. princesses
3. horses
4. mushrooms
5. watches
6. shovels
7. axes
8. tubas
9. mammals
10. peaches
11. giraffes
12. hotels
13. dolphins
14. sandwiches
15. wishes
16. carrots
17. alligators
18. candies
19. bandages
20. arrows

Answer Pages

Page 14
1. geese   2. wolves   3. buffalo
4. mice   5. sheep   6. elk
7. oxen   8. fish

Page 15
1. Australia, (kangaroos) (animals) (legs)
2. (kangaroos) New Guinea
3. (kangaroos) (leaves)
4. (people,) New Zealand, Matt
5. Australia
   ("they" can be circled, but not required at this point)
6. Matt, (children) (kangaroos)
7. (kangaroos) (heads) (deer) (legs) (rabbits)
8. Simpson Desert, Matt, (kangaroos)
9. Murray River, (kangaroos)
10. (babies) (mothers') (pouches)
11. Sydney, Matt, (parents) (kangaroos)

Page 16
Answers will vary.

Page 17
1. is   2. is   3. was
4. am   5. are/were   6. were
7. is   8. is   9. are/were
10. was   11. am/was

Page 18
1. have   2. was   3. are
4. is   5. can/do   6. do/can
7. does   8. am   9. would/might
10. might

Page 19
1. studied   2. learned   3. discovered
4. cooked   5. carried   6. regulated
7. invented   8. mixed

Page 20
was, heard, did, wrote, gave, took
thought, told, began, gave

Page 21
1. brings   2. call   3. hangs
4. say   5. link   6. take
7. moves   8. allows   9. grows
10. bend   11. shakes

Page 22
1. dragged   2. invented   3. appeared
4. began   5. is   6. help
7. are   8. is

Page 23
friend's, house's, dad's
Andrea's, flashlight's, door's
Other answers will vary.

Page 24
1. They   2. She   3. our
4. He   5. we   6. She
7. It   8. We   9. They
10. We   11. She   12. he

Page 25
them, him, her, it
them, him
us, me
you

Page 26
1. my   2. Her   3. its
4. My   5. my   6. her
7. his   8. my   9. their
10. My   11. our   12. your

Page 27
1. they, its   2. he, us   3. we, it
   Julie and Jake were the first student astronauts, and they went into the spaceship.

Page 28
1. young, famous   2. wonderful
3. Many, perfect   4. brilliant, scary
5. exciting   6. funny, imaginative
7. favorite   8. important, little, pleasant
9. humorous, serious, memorable

Page 29
1. ugliest   2. high   3. higher
4. highest   5. farther   6. fastest
7. dirtier   8. hardest

page 30
These are possible answers, though answers may vary.
1. brightly   2. quickly   3. timidly
4. heavily   5. wildly   6. loudly
7. quietly   8. carefully

Page 31
1. good   2. well   3. good
4. good   5. well   6. good
7. well   8. good   9. good

Page 32
1. an   2. a   3. an   4. a
5. a   6. an   7. a   8. a

© Rainbow Bridge Publishing   www.rbpbooks.com   reproducible   **MBS—Grammar Grade 3**

Answer Pages

Page 33
1. any   2. no   3. none
4. any   5. no   6. anything
7. no one   8. no   9. a
10. any

Page 34
yell, complain, big, flame, inexpensive, small, chide, assist, name, glimmer

Page 35
kind, loved, quiet, young, boy
friend
Yes, do
brave, stay
good, excellent
smiled, always

Page 36
1. to   2. step, way   3. capitol
4. principal   5. Their, sun   6. there
7. blew   8. You're   9. It's

Page 37
Davy Crockett in Tennessee in 1876.
Parents very glad.
Elected to Congress.
When he was almost fifty years old.
Met two other famous men, Jim Bowie and William Travis.
The battle thirteen days.

Page 38
1. Kites
2. China, kites
3. soldiers
4. kite
5. Children, Europe
6. kite
7. frames
8. triangles
9. England, person

Page 39
The following should be capitalized:
George, Jessica, Mountview Elementary School, Asia, Mount Fuji, Eskimo, White House, James Cook, Virginia, Zeus.
Plurals:
women, foxes, pencils, catches, deer, wolves, shelves, glasses, vases.

Page 40
1. like   2. enjoyed   3. were
4. represented   5. are   6. tries
7. gather   8. Running   9. balance
10. compete   11. operates   12. won

Page 41
1. says
2. Astronomers, believe
3. name, has
4. were
5. Planets, are, objects, revolve
   planet, is, object, revolves
6. is
7. moves

Page 42
1. Americans like hamburgers; they consume...
2. In New Zealand, they made the world's biggest cookie.
3. It was big enough to cover two tennis courts.
4. George Crum was an American Indian, and he invented potato chips.
5. In Japan, people eat raw fish, and they love it.
6. Pizza is my sister's favorite, and she even eats it for breakfast.

Page 43
1. smaller   2. largest   3. more
4. densely   5. well   6. hardest
7. happily   8. quietly   9. pretty
10. carefully   11. good   12. fastest

Page 44
Answers will vary, but the sentences should be complete, and the story should include at least one statement, one question, one exclamation and one command.

Page 45
Answers will vary.